The
Power Of
Habit
Second Edition

Benjamin A. Chapin
www.benjaminchapin.com

DEDICATION

Dedicated to my father.
The man who taught me to think deeply and reflect daily.

CONTENTS

ACKNOWLEDGMENTS

First and foremost, I want to thank God. God's salvation through the death, burial and resurrection of Jesus Christ gives us all the ability to have a personal relationship with the creator of the Universe.

I also want to thank my wife. She's my muse and my inspiration. A wonderful wife, an amazing mother and the best person I have ever met. She's great and has always stood by me with every decision I have made along life's way.

I'd like to thank my editors and early readers for helping me along the way. I also want to thank all of my friends and extended family for the support. It's a true blessing to have every person I know in my life.

INTRODUCTION

A person is an accumulation of experiences that have led them to who they are today. People are faced with decisions on what to wear, what to eat, who to date, where to work and so on. The choices we make today will shape how to tomorrow will unfold. Habits play a vital and strong role in your daily decisions and in this book, you'll learn how.

With a life super charged by habits, it's important not only to learn how strong of a role they play in our life, but in the lives of those around us. Our daily habits affect the way we speak and interact with other people, the way we eat and sleep and even the way we drive. With so many different avenues in life affected by our habits, it's vital to have a way to adapt to change in our habits. This book is going to help you adapt to the new habits you are attempting to implement and transform the bad and negative habits you once had.

The power that is within our habits is deep below the surface. While the majority of people are aware that good habits are good to have, they are not aware how deeply rooted our habits are in our lives. Once you begin to dig deep and discover your true habits and the power you have, you'll be able to achieve anything you wish to achieve.

One of the most fundamental building blocks in building good habits is self reflection. Being able to stop looking at others and turning that onto yourself, you'll be able to get to know yourself a little bit better and discover some things you might never have known otherwise. When we know more of the "how" we are able to determine better the "why."

There are many books out on habit, but the other books spend a large amount of time on case studies and other people's experiences out in the world with breaking bad habits and forming new ones. I did not want to take that approach with this book, someone in a case study is not you, and it's someone in a case study!

Instead, I want to give you real applicable advice on how to make some adjustments in your own life on your daily habits. I have mastered habits and now live daily using them to my full advantage. With a family, a full time job, writing & a couple different online business ventures, I had to learn the art of balance. With that balance comes my daily habits.

I am going to give you what I've done in my own life and the hope is it helps you in your own personal life. There won't be case studies or discussion on different medical related reasons on how habits form and break. This is real advice from someone who's been there.

If you wish to change your habits into habits that work for you and unlock the power of habit, I'd keep reading and hold on tight. My desire is you can experience this book and enjoy it, then go practice it. Habits take thirty days to develop, with this book; you can get started developing those habits starting today.

THE HABITUAL LIFESTYLE
DISCOVERED

"We become what we repeatedly do." ~ Sean Covey

Each person has a set of habits. Many people might not notice many of the habits they already have. For example, when you awake in the morning do you do a specific set of tasks? For myself, I always jolt myself out of bed and go put on coffee and then I proceed to the shower. Others have variations, but the habits are there.

Finding your habits you already have can help shape your understanding of how your habits work. The habits vary in size, length and repetition, but one consistency between all of them is the fact they are continually repeated. This repetition and pattern that we create in our habits help automate tasks. This automation process simplifies the task for our mind; a great example of this would be walking.

How often do you need to think to walk? If you are like most people, you don't at all. When we were very small and learning to walk, we had to think and concentrate on the process of walking in much more care and detail than we do today. While we do "learn" to walk, we also create a habit inside our muscles and brains that allows us to walk. That's why some people after a bad accident need to re-learn walking; something went wrong inside their mind.

If you have a morning routine setup and then proceed to move to a new house, all those habits and routines take a little time to get resynced and put into place. Oftentimes, you'll find yourself more tired after you move living locations, not because of the physical toll on your body, but because of the new habits that need to form. Changes in the habits we have require us to use more energy because the task is changing and requiring more of our mind.

The more habits we have that are systematic and automated, the less we need to think about the tasks that are assigned inside of those habits. The less we think about the tasks, the less toll it takes on our mind. Our mind is processing large amounts of data, making split second decisions and pretty much running the show. There is so much going on that anything the mind can organize into a repetitive habit, it will take advantage and do so.

This saves our brain processing power on these mundane tasks and lets the mind focus on what is more important. Automating tasks in our everyday lives can seem daunting and un-needed, but the benefits are supreme. As mentioned earlier, you probably already have a list of habits you have. Habits are either a good or bad habit, there is not much gray area in between because it is either helpful to your life to have that habit or it is not.

Identifying the good habits can take a little bit of digging if you are to find each one in your daily routines. The good habits in life are habits that increase your life value; they add value by automating successful and positive habits that are helpful. It does not matter what time of the day the habits are taking place, just the fact that they exist to benefit your life in a good way.

Identifying bad habits is a little bit easier to notice, they consist of repetitious bad behaviors. How do we declare what "bad" is? For this book, the word "bad" will represent anything that is not beneficial to our lives or our minds. The mind after all, is the most precious item we will ever acquire in this life and we did not have to pay a single penny to acquire it.

Our habits in life shape our reality and reflect our mental health on a daily basis. It is only when we are able to identify, adjust, and change our habits that we can release the true power that is within each habit. Habits are like toothbrushes, they only work when you know how to use them properly.

The power that is inside each habit will be explained throughout the entirety of this book, but will not be outright identified. You might already know the power of habit, you might find it with one of the chapters in this book or you might not know the power of habit until you have read the book in its entirety twice over. Regardless of when you discover what the power of habit is, you will know it like a giant light bulb just went off in your head.

With the knowledge and insight into the power of habit plus knowing what to do with it by reading this book, you will have unlimited possibilities for your life. You will be able to change and manage your time efficiently; you'll be able to spend time with loved ones more often and yet still put in incredible amounts of work.

How can it be possible that you work extremely hard

but also have time for family? It has to do with your habits and how the habits in your life are functioning. A poorly functioning habit will not serve you much use in daily life, but instead it will hold you back from achieving your desired results and outcomes. The habits you have will make and break every dream, desire and goal you ever had. Without good habits, goals are merely day dreams you ponder as you take a nap in your lazy boy chair.

Without the power of habit in your life, you cannot progress in a forward motion. That momentum to move forward has to be directed in your mind, the mind needs all the room it can have in order to think clearly and accurately, so automated good habits will help steer the life you live in the right direction.

A life were you work hard and play hard without draining your energy levels to zilch, sounds like a fairy tale doesn't it? I thought so until I discovered the power of habits. That power has the ability to change lives like never before seen. No longer will you struggle with the lack of hours in the day, the chaos in the world and stress on family dynamics. It can all be done away with when you adapt the power you have in your habits.

Discovering how your habits are formed and where they already exist in your life is the first step in harnessing the power. Identify each habit you have and by doing so, you will find where the most powerful spots in the day are to form new habits. This might sound complicated at first, but as you journey down the path you will understand more.

Morning people tend to have the most productive habits in the first parts of the day, while night owls find themselves more productive and energized in the evenings. Attempting to force yourself into productive habits in areas of the day you are not naturally energized can keep you from maximizing their efficiency.

Instead of forcing yourself to develop productive habits in the evening when you are a morning person, develop your habits in the earlier part of the day. That might require some sacrifice on sleep, but the energized levels you have in the morning will increase your productivity in your habits and will prove more useful than attempting to form them in the evenings.

If you wish to become a morning person or an evening person, you have to ease yourself into it. People often have the absolute truth about themselves that they are not a "morning person" or a "night person" and stick strong to that truth. While they might not be that role today, with enough time and habit investment, they could change over the course of time.

This change of habit is similar to changing jobs, moving or any other dramatic change, it takes time and repetition for it to work. If Frank gets a new job across town and has to leave early by twenty minutes, he'll need to leave early at the same time every day. Eventually, it'll become part of his natural process. This example is simple, but exactly like attempting to make a change of habit such as changing from a night person to a morning person, small steps with the end result in mind proves to be successful while a large burst falls flat.

All habits take time and patience to develop into success. This concept of "patience" and "waiting" is virtually unknown by the vast majority of today's culture. Any given person is upset if a web page takes more than a few moments to load, let alone a month for a good habit to form. Developing the ability to have patience is important when forming new habits and making adjustments to old ones.

The power of habit is a secret that not many know, but many practice. With the knowledge and the ability to shed away absolute truths about ourselves such as "being a night owl", we are able to tap into this power of habit and unlock what life truly has to offer.

Questions & Answers

What habit(s) can you think of that are productive and healthy in your life?

_____

_____

_____

_____

_____

What habit(s) can you think of that are unhealthy and destructive that you have?

_____

_____

_____

_____

_____

Are you willing to make changes in your unhealthy habit(s)? Why or why not?

_____

_____

_____

_____

_____

SECTION 1: PHYSICAL HABITS

People often say there isn't enough time in the day to get everything accomplished. But everyone has the same 24 hour day as everyone else; it's what people choose to do with them that show one's priorities. One can choose to be a couch potato and waste away their life, or one can choose to exercise, eat right, and enjoy every day to its fullest by feeling the best and being the best.

I hope you chose to be the best you can be, and chose to develop healthier habits that will stick with you for a life time. In the chapter that follows, I'll show an example of a healthy habit called "The 4'oclock Start Habit". Its design is to give you a little more time in the day for what is important to you, but realistically it is not for everyone. It is just an example of where you can find that extra time to implement your new habit, like exercising each day. Find out what works for you and go from there.

THE 4'OCLOCK START HABIT

"It is well to be up before daybreak, for such habits contribute to health, wealth, and wisdom." ~ Aristotle

We live extremely busy lives that pull us in multiple directions on a daily basis. What if we were able to have an extra couple hours every morning? Before the world wakes up and starts to demand our time, what if we could somehow find extra time before that?

If you are like most people, including myself, 4 am is reserved for sleep. There is no way on earth I want to be up at 4'oclock in the morning! While it can be painful, the usefulness of the 4am start is beyond measure. If you look at successful people and their habits, an early start is one of their habits.

If you are in a race and you are able to get off the line before everyone else that gives you an advantage. Essentially, the 4am start to the day gives you a head start on the day. No more worries about trying to find a couple minutes here and there to fit in some extra work for your side projects, no more wondering how you'll find time to do this or that. The 4am start gives you everything you need.

When I began getting up earlier, I began slowly. I usually would get up at 6:30 am in order to make it to work at 8am. I set my alarm to 6 am in order to test the waters; that was a very easy adjustment. So I set it back to 5:30 am, that wasn't too bad either. What I discovered when I began setting my alarm back more and more that I was creating time for myself and whatever I needed to accomplish. So I got a little addicted; kept getting use to times and setting it back more and more.

When I set my alarm for 4:30 am, it was insane. I had 3 ½ hours of free time alone before I went to work. I couldn't believe it. 4:30 am was uncomfortable, but I wanted more, so I went ahead and did 4am. That's when I realized 4 am was the mark I needed to stick at. It was uncomfortable and painful...sometimes still is. I usually get to bed around 10 pm, so I get 6 hours of sleep every night. I have 4 hours in the morning to work and do as I please. Some days I work on writing, other days marketing, just depends on what I decide.

If you were to wake up 1 hour earlier each day for a year, you would have over an additional 15 days in the year. If you were to wake up 2 hours early, you would have over a month extra in your calendar year. People are very concerned about how limited their time is and when they do find time to work, it's often full of interruptions.

If you want to life hack and get some more productivity out of your life, it's worth looking into waking up earlier. You can start slow like I did or you can try to push hard right out the gate. I'll warn you, if you try to rush the process of developing a good habit, you are more likely to fall right on your face. Instead, pace yourself and allow the excellent habit to take form properly.

When you embrace a 4'oclock start habit, you unlock your life in a way that most people will never understand. Not only do you get more work done, you are able to spend the other hours in the day with the people that matter most to you. A happy and successful life is not about how much money you have in the bank, it's about the relationships you have and your ability to help keep them nurtured and happy. Even if you do not want to be more productive or have side projects, just having extra time in life is great to have.

Discover the freedom of the 4'oclock start and give it a shot. You might just end up enjoying it more than you think.

For those who need a visual here is an example of The 4'oclock Start Habit:

Step 1: Chart Your Time

Organize your time in the day as best as you can, try to account for every hour. Here's an example to help you.

12 am – 7 am – Sleeping

7 am – 8 am – Getting Ready for Work

8 am – 5 pm – Working

5 pm – 6 pm – Driving Home, Eating Dinner

6 pm – 10 pm – TV, Video Games, Family

10 pm – 12 am – Sleeping

You do not need to be specific such as the time you go to the bathroom and how long you are in the shower. Just a rough outline of what your day looks like will do the trick.

Step 2: Identifying the Sacrifice

In order to create time you either need to add hours to the 24 hour clock or you will need to find areas of time in your day you can reduce. The best way to do this is to determine what can be reduced and/or eliminated.

12am – 7am – Sleeping
10pm – 12am – Sleeping

Sleeping is an easy target to reduce. This individual for the example is getting 9 hours of sleep a night. Remember, you have to SACRIFICE in order to get some extra hours in the day.

6pm-10pm – TV, Video Games, Family

Another possible avenue would be this area. It can be tricky because family structure and maintaining family bonding time is important. You do not want to mess with the relationships and the people you love in order to find time. Sometimes sacrifice is needed, but oftentimes it can be found elsewhere. The fact remains, you have to sacrifice something in your day in order to gain additional time.

Step 3: Baby Steps

The natural route at this point would be to start slashing all the areas you want to sacrifice. While it sounds great in theory, you will be burnt out very quickly. Instead, take some small steps in the right direction.

10pm – 7am – Sleeping
Baby Step into…
10pm – 6am – Sleeping

And…
6pm-10pm – TV, Video Games, Family
Baby Step into…
6pm-9pm – TV, Video Games, Family

With these small changes you have gained yourself 2 hours! That's an extra 30.4 days of time a year! What could you do with 30 days extra a year? These two small baby steps net you a load of time!

Step 4: Rinse & Repeat

In order to form this into a habit, you will need to adapt this to daily life. That means sticking to it no matter what. Oftentimes, people sleep in on the weekends which is a big no-no when you are attempting to form a habit.

Remember, habits are supposed to be something that naturally happens with little to no thought eventually. If you sleep in on the weekends, it will make getting up early on the weekdays difficult and a burden.

Step 5: Adjust

As your habits grow and develop, you will want to revisit them and adjust them accordingly. For instance, the example individual we used might want to go back and adjust a little more, maybe another hour off of sleeping and TV time to give himself another 30.4 days, making a total of 60 days or two months!

You have the power to change and create new habits in

your life. Creating time is a small habit that can be done easily when adapted and instituted properly.

Game Plan for Time Creation

Step 1: Identify Where You Spend Time

Step 2: Identify Areas for Reducing Time

Step 3: Take Small Steps in the Right Direction

Step 4: Form the Habit by Repetition

Step 5: Make Adjustments When Needed

Questions & Answers

Do you think you have good exercise and eating habits?

_____

_____

_____

_____

_____

Do you think The 4'Oclock habit or an adaptation of it might work for you?

_____

_____

_____

_____

_____

Take time and write down what you think you need to improve on with eating and exercising, and continue to add to the list as you read on.

_____

_____

_____

_____

_____

EXERCISE HABITS

Exercise is so important for a person's mind and body. Starting an exercise routine is a great healthy habit to develop, and keeping with it is one of the best habits you can do for yourself. *Note, if you haven't been active, have any health problems, if you're pregnant or an older adult please speak with your doctor before starting any rigorous exercise.*

We've previously talked about MAKING time for what is important, so with an idea of *when* already in our minds, we can focus on *how* we will build this habit. If you exercise at the same time every day it is more likely to stick as a habit, so if it is possible try to keep to that time. If not, sneak it in whenever you can.

When implementing an exercise routine, start slowly and build up to your ideal goal. Most people should get in between 30-60 minutes a day, 5 times a week. So start off walking 20 minutes, then increase as you go. If someone is willing to come along on your walk/exercise routine then it is very helpful because it is a great way to stay the course. Plus I find it passes the time quicker. Do not stop exercising if you get bored; just vary your work out. Don't feel hopeless when you are out of breath easily at first, endurance will come to you as your exercising habit progresses. Make it fun, and this routine will become a healthy habit in no time.

The benefits of regular exercise are amazing. It helps you sleep better, increases your energy and endurance and helps relieve depression, stress, and anxiety. It can reduce some effects of aging, especially the discomfort of osteoarthritis while also contributing to mental well-being. Studies have shown exercise furthermore reduces your risk of heart disease, high blood pressure, osteoporosis, diabetes, and obesity. Not to mention it helps you maintain a normal weight by increasing your metabolism and burning those extra calories. With those perks this is one habit you want to start right away!

While exercising it is a good idea to find your target heart rate. To check your heart rate you lightly press the tips of your first 2 fingers on the inside of your wrist. Count your pulse for 15 seconds, and multiply the number by 4. Use your phone to time the 15 seconds so it's most accurate. The goal is to keep your heart rate between 50% and 85% of their maximum heart rate when exercising to gain the most benefit from it. To figure out your maximum heart rate, subtract your age (in years) from 220. This number is your maximum heart rate. To figure out your target heart rate range, multiply that number by 0.50 and 0.85.

Example for a 30 year old:

Maximum HR	50% of Maximum	85% of Maximum
220 − 30 = **190**	190 x 0.50 = **95**	190 x 0.85 = **161.5**

So for a 30 year old their target heart range is between 95 and 161.5. When you first start developing your habit of exercising, try and aim for the lower end of your target heart range. As you progress in your exercise program, build up to the higher end of the target heart range. This will make sure you stay safe and don't overdo it while you work out.

This is an exercise plan that works for me and keeps me interested. Find out what you like most and your body responds to and go with it. Here's the schedule I started with and what it transitioned into.

First Week:
Cardio* – Bike/elliptical – 1 x hour – keeping pulse above 140
Frequency: Daily (30-45 minutes AM/ 30 minutes PM) alternate bike/elliptical every other day

Strength – Circuit Training (works all muscles through various stations)
Frequency: Every Other Day (time: 30-45 minutes)

Second Week:
Cardio* – Elliptical – 30 minutes – keeping pulse above 145
Frequency: Mon/Wed/Fri

Strength – Circuit Training (works all muscles through various stations)
Frequency: Mon/Wed/Fri

Abs – 3 x 10 – various ab exercises to work core

*Note about cardio workouts – I use HIIT technique when doing cardio. It stands for High Intensity Interval Training and basically what it means is during the work out

I have periods I push myself to the max for a short while and then back down to a normal exercise level. I find this to be helpful.

These work outs and whatnot will change from week to week to create "muscle confusion". This confusion of the muscles helps keep the muscles guessing what's next and will maximize the work outs. It also gives your muscles time to heal the tissue that was torn during your workout. If you do the same workout everyday it won't give your muscles time to heal, which leaves you open to injury. A great idea to make exercise a little more interesting would be to put your elliptical in front of your TV, and watch the news, a show, or a movie to keep you occupied. I've found if I am distracted while working out then it passes by a little faster and it keeps me from stopping earlier then my goal. Some people would rather listen to music, find something to keep you going once you start and stick with it.

Things to remember once exercise is a daily habit for you include getting enough water, getting enough sleep and don't forget to stretch before you exercise. It is important to get enough water while exercising because it is crucial so your body doesn't conserve water, and keep you from giving off heat through sweat. Drink 16oz before your work out, about 5oz every 20 minutes while working out, and then top it off with even more water when you are done. Make sure you get plenty of sleep at night so that your body can release growth hormones and repair the trauma done to your muscles that day. Try to get at least 6 hours of sleep each night. Lastly, stretching before your work out will prepare your muscles for the exercise, and stretching after it will improve your flexibility. Holding each stretch for only 10 seconds is enough time to get the results. Hopefully these helpful hints will guide you into approaching this habit the correct way for lasting impact.

Regardless of which exercises you chose to implement, incorporating daily movement is one habit closer to being a better you. Even doing some stretches while you watch TV is better than just sitting on the couch. There are many creative ways to throw in a little extra to your day and get your body moving that people don't even realize. Take the stairs instead of the elevator/ escalator. This little act can go a long ways in improving your heart and lower cholesterol with only as little as 2 minutes several times a day. Work outside your house in your garden, yard, etc. While doing household work pick up your pace and get your heart rate up a bit. Instead of sitting in the break room at work, go for a walk during your coffee break or lunch break. While running errands try to park your vehicle further away from the entrance at stores or restaurants. And lastly a creative way to add some exercise into your day would be to walk all (or part of) the way to work instead of driving. This isn't always possible, but if you can do it once in a while try to.

When done correctly, there is no downside to adding the habit of exercise to your life. There are only benefits and a better version of you.

Questions & Answers

When is a good time every day for you to exercise?

_____

_____

_____

_____

_____

Write down some people you know who might exercise with you.

_____

_____

_____

_____

_____

Can you identify some daily tasks you can do different to sneak exercise in?

_____

_____

_____

_____

_____

EATING HABITS

"You are what you eat." ~ Everybody's Mom

Food is amazing. There are so many different kinds of foods, different tastes; and different cultures even have different ways of cooking things. It's no wonder that we have certain eating habits and do not even realize it. We have had them so long they are a part of our daily life and we don't think about them, but we need to and need to make sure they are good eating habits. Good habits make sure our bodies get the energy we need to function.

Most people can look at what they eat each day and see where they can improve. Eating habits are ingrained in us at a very young age. We snack on what we snacked on as kids, we cook what we saw our parents cooking, and we buy what we've always bought. In times of stress we fall back on what is comforting which are old habits mostly associated with eating. But this is not healthy and it is not ok.

You have to figure out which bad eating habits you have (i.e. chocolate after that stressful meeting) and then figure out how to SLOWLY get rid of them. You can try going cold turkey, or you can implement a healthy life style over a month. Take small steps like starting with a healthy breakfast for a week, then breakfast and lunch being healthy the next week. The week after that grab a smaller portion at dinner instead of that extra-large one you're used to. After a couple weeks of healthy breakfast and lunches and smaller portions transition to a healthy dinner. Snacks are up to each individual, but fruits and vegetables are great ideas in between meals to curb your hunger. My daughter loves celery with some peanut butter to dunk them into. You can even add a few raisins to make them even tastier which is called Ants on a Log. For the recipe see the end of this chapter.

To make sure you don't fall back on old bad habits you must also work on stress management. Eating when you are stressed doesn't accomplish anything productive with your stress; it actually will just make you feel worse in the long run. Figure out a different outlet for your stress, like exercise (my favorite), relaxation, meditation etc. Find what works for you, keeps you interested and makes you feel good. Not only will your waistline appreciate your new stress cooping strategy, but you will feel so much better if you make the change.

What you eat also affects your body and attitude. Nutrients give your body instructions about how to function, so eating healthy foods packed with nutrients is very important. Unhealthy foods lack nutrients and some even have chemically-altered fats and sugars that give our bodies the wrong signals. Healthy diets have even shown to help learning and memory in people with depression, schizophrenia and Alzheimer's. It is so important to control what you eat for overall health.

Living healthy is a combination of diet adjustment and exercise for optimal health. In the previous chapter we spoke on the importance of exercise and the role it plays with our body, and now we have talked about how food affects our body. Here are a few steps you can take to implement the healthy habits we've talked about in the section of physical habits.

Step 1: Fix Eating

You can exercise until you are blue in the face every single day but not make much progress if you do not adjust the eating habits you have. You have to be real and honest in identifying the troublesome areas in your eating habits.

Some people find it helpful to visually see problem areas; one way is to start by writing a list of food(s) you should not be eating. Here is a list of snacks that are not a good choice for your healthy eating habit:

ChipsCandy
Soda
Cookies
Cake
Brownies
Fudge

Anything that comes to mind that you are consuming that is high in sugar, high in carbs, high in sodium or just not benefiting you should be listed. The above list is an example of what not to eat, so then make another list of healthier items you like and could eat instead for example:

Bananas and peanut butter
Grapefruit
Celery and peanut better
Carrots
Strawberries

Take that second list of good foods and add it to your grocery list. Keeping healthy food in your house readily available will decrease temptation of eating the wrong kinds of food. You can use this same method that we used on snacks for meals that are not healthy and meals that are. Listing them out not only makes you realize how much you can change up your eating habits, but it also will help you have ideas already written down for healthy dinners to meal plan with. Please see the end of this chapter for the recipe "Southwestern Stuffed Peppers". It's a yummy, healthy recipe sure to make the family happy.

Step 2: Design a Workout Regiment

We talked about the importance of exercise previously, but let me again point out its importance for overall health. You will feel so much better if you combine the healthy eating and exercise habits. You will be your 100%. Be sure to stretch before and after exercise, alternate exercises and monitor your heart rate during the exercise.

Step 3: Cheat Days (Optional for some, required for others)

I've tried to eat proper and live a perfect life before and have always failed shortly after starting because I love delicious food. I found that adding a "cheat day" or 1 or 2 "cheat meals" to the mix really helped me. Date night, BBQ at work, etc… are times I'll cheat on my diet and I've still managed to see results in the end. The goal is to live a healthier life, but you also want to enjoy life and sometimes occasions are special and you want to eat the cake for your wedding anniversary. That is okay, and doesn't mean you need to stop your new habit of healthy eating because of one cheat snack. Enjoy your slice of cake, and then go back to eating the right foods.

Step 4: Obsession to Habit

When you take your body and tell it to work hard, it's going to have a natural tendency to avoid it because it doesn't feel good. If you are like me and have spent years not doing much fitness your body identifies working out and sweating as negative and will want to avoid it.

Obsessing over fitness and health for the first while is going to help create the long lasting habit that you desire to have. Once you get over that initial reluctance from your body, the exercise will feel amazing and you will almost crave it. And once you eat healthy and find some healthy foods you enjoy it will be that much easier!

<u>Game Plan for Healthy Living</u>

Step 1: Remove Bad Eating Habits

Step 2: Increase Healthy Food Intake

Step 3: Have a Cheat Day or Meal(s)

Step 4: Exercise with a Combination of Cardio and Strength Training

Step 5: Obsess Over Healthy Living Until You Have a Habit

Here are a couple healthy recipes for those starting their healthy eating journey. Hope you enjoy.

<u>Southwestern Stuffed Peppers</u>

Serves 4
Preparation: 10 minutes
Cooking Time: 80 minutes

Ingredients
1 cup long-grain white rice
1 tablespoon olive oil
6 scallions, thinly sliced, white and green parts separated
½ pound ground beef chuck
1 cup frozen corn
14.5 ounce can chopped green chilies
1 teaspoon ground cumin
4 ounces Monterey jack, grated (1cup)
Kosher salt and black pepper
4 large bell peppers, halved lengthwise, ribs and seeds removed
½ cup plain low-fat Greek yogurt
Salsa- for serving

Directions
1.   Heat oven to 375 degrees F. Cook the rice according to the package directions.

2.   Heat the oil in a large skillet over medium-high heat. Add the scallion whites and beef and cook, breaking the beef up with a spoon, until no longer pink, 3 to 5 minutes. Stir in the corn, chilies, cumin, cooked rice, ½ cup of the Monterey jack, ½ teaspoon salt, and ¼ teaspoon black pepper.

3.   Arrange the bell peppers, cut-side up, in a 9-by-

13-inch baking dish or pan. Divide the beef mixture among the bell peppers, add ½ cup water to the dish, tightly cover the dish with foil, and bake until the bell peppers are soft, 30 to 40 minutes. Uncover, sprinkle with the remaining ½ cup of Monterey jack, and bake until browned, 5 to 7 minutes more.

4.   In a small bowl, whisk together the yogurt and ¼ cup water. Drizzle over the bell peppers and top with the salsa and scallion greens.

5.   Serve immediately.

Note: for an even healthier option you can substitute the ground beef for ground turkey.

Ants on a log

Ingredients
5 stalks celery
½ cup peanut butter
¼ cup raisins

Directions
1. Cut the celery stalks in half.
2. Spread with peanut butter.
3. Sprinkle with raisins.
4. Enjoy! Easy healthy snack for all ages

Peanut Butter Toast Delight

Ingredients
Peanut butter
Toast
Thinly sliced apples or bananas
Cinnamon

Directions
1. Toast the bread
2. Spread with peanut butter.
3. Add pieces of fruit
4. Sprinkle cinnamon over top
5. Microwave for 15 seconds

Or

1. Assemble the above then toast in oven

Questions & Answers:

Which step of Healthy Living will you find easiest?

_____

_____

_____

_____

_____

Which step will you find hardest?

_____

_____

_____

_____

_____

What is your game plan to power through that tough step towards healthy living?

_____

_____

_____

_____

_____

Here are some things I want you to do:
Name a few recipes you love.

_____

_____

_____

_____

_____

Identify ways you can substitute ingredients to make them healthier.

_____

_____

_____

_____

_____

Look up and make at least one new healthy recipe each week and save it (if you like it).

SUMMARY OF SECTION 1

Taking care of your body is the best thing you could do for yourself. Exercising and eating healthy are THE habits to implement. Once you have switched old eating habits into healthier ones and added exercise into your life you will reap the benefits right away. Eating right and exercising regularly controls your weight so you don't gain, and it improves your mood with the chemicals your brain lets off.

These new habits will also help you fight off and prevent diseases like stroke, high blood pressure and heart disease. And lastly, eating healthy and exercising will boost your energy and improves your chance at a longer life. So take those stairs and choose the chicken over ground beef next time you are out. It's the little habit changes added up that can make the most difference sometimes.

SECTION 2: RELATIONAL HABITS

"Nothing so needs reforming as other people's habits." ~ *Mark Twain*

Changing your own bad habits into good ones is the most important step to having healthy relational habits with your friends, coworkers and loved ones. It's the ground work so-to-speak. After you are the best you can be, other good habits will fall more easily into place.

Instead of eating horribly and feeling like crud afterwards, you chose to eat healthy and now have more energy to play at the park with your kids. Instead of staying up late playing video games you chose to get some sleep, and therefore can give your 100% at work the next day. Instead of waking up and watching TV you walked an hour on the treadmill while watching TV, which boosted your endorphins and now you are happier and your spouse appreciates your new attitude on life. If you focus on yourself first, your relationships will be that much easier to make right.

Others will notice the change and hopefully be happy for you, but they might be upset by your decisions which can be an expected result. Anytime there is a change, especially in bad habits that you are not participating in anymore, people will take notice. Other people know they are bad habits but refuse to change and you will be a constant reminder they could do better and haven't. They will be negative, but just ignore them. Do not be alarmed, but continue on with your adjustments and new habits.

When you identify and proceed to eliminate or adjust bad habits in life, you will begin to notice other people's bad habits. The first reaction you will have when this begins is to let them know what they are doing wrong and how they can fix it. While in theory this sounds great, the result is horrible. Trust me, I've been there. Do not try to fix other people; they do not want to be fixed or made aware of what they might be doing wrong.

The alternative you should opt for would be to lead by example. Others will take notice of the changes you are making and if the changes are impressive, they will eventually begin to ask what the heck is going on. When they start asking questions, that is the time you will be able to give them your insight and knowledge. This approach is more easily received, but sometimes still will fall on deaf ears. So stay your course, and regardless how other people take it, keep on keeping on.

People make choices every single day, some of the choices they are fully aware of. Other choices they are not aware of, but can be made aware of. The habits we partake in are often in the latter, they are the choices we are not aware of but can be made aware of. Knowledge is power and knowing that our bad habits are holding us back from achieving what we wish to achieve in life is going to equip us with eyes that see more clearly into our own lives.

When you begin to analyze your bad habits that are present in your life, they will overlay with other people's bad habits. That is the reason why it was earlier explained to ignore others' bad habits unless they approach you. As you process your habits, do not downplay or make small the bad and toxic habits that exist. Minimizing your bad habits only makes you feel good, it does not solve any issues. Being honest and acknowledging the problematic areas of your life will give you the power and direction that you desire for the life you live.

In this section we will focus on your habits with the people around you, since you have mastered your personal habits in the previous section.

Questions & Answers

What do you think you could do better in your relationship with your spouse?

_____

_____

_____

_____

_____

Which habits do you think need to change with how you relate to your family?

_____

_____

_____

_____

_____

What are some habits you can implement today that will progress your work life?

_____

_____

_____

_____

_____

MARTIAL HABITS

Relationships can blossom and marriages can be saved by instituting some good habits into the mix. If a spouse feels their significant other is neglectful or uncaring but then all of a sudden starts engaging more on a consistent basis, it can work miracles and change lives.

No one gets married thinking about it ending. Everyone wants it to work, and one way to help it work is developing healthy happy habits with your spouse. Its recognizing the good ones you already have in place, and eliminating the bad ones completely if possible. Sometimes it can even be changing one part of a bad habit and making it a good one.

For example, watching Television is a bad habit that is common. It can cause you to ignore things that need to be done, people who need attention, and your spouse while they are trying to talk to you. The habitual lifestyle of television junkies is powerful and has been destroying productive lives since the television has been invented.

Before you think I do not watch television, let me

clarify I do. I do so in moderation and I do so with my wife. We have a couple shows and it makes my wife feel good for us to sit down and watch them and throughout the week discuss them. At one point, I banned television watching for myself, but it did not work out so well since it was something my wife and I did together. While the habit is not great, I had to make a mental adjustment.

I see the time I spend with my wife watching television as time we are sharing together and it makes what once was a bad habit into a good habit because it is time together. It is adjustments like this that will allow us to not break everyone's spirit around us as we make these dramatic shifts in our life.

Other good habits to try implementing into your marriage include but aren't limited to:

~ Avoiding grudges by keeping short accounts with each other
~ Always siding with each other
~ Flirting with each other
~ Ask the question "does it really matter?" before reacting to arguments
~ Treat each other as if today were the last
~ Be willing to say sorry and ask forgiveness
~ Place a high priority on having fun with each other

This list could also be considered advice for a good relationship. Taking advice and sticking with it is the exact same thing as a habit. If you take the bad habit of flirting with random strangers for the thrill, and instead apply your flirting skills to flirting with your spouse only, then your relationship will prosper. Your spouse will flourish under the attention, as most people enjoy being recognized and admired. Habits come in many forms, recognizing them and keeping good ones will go a long way towards that ideal relationship.

My mom gave me some advice when I got married: never go to bed without at least touching your spouse that day. Whether it be a kiss, hug, or a high five make that connection with your spouse to keep it real between each other. Humans need physical contact; it is one of our most basic needs! Without it someone can feel very lonely so make the extra effort to touch your spouse.

On that note, one other way to improve your marriage is keeping up the habit of having sex with your spouse. It will help you keep the connection; help both of you feel loved, and bonds you closer each time. Other surprising benefits of sex include a boosted immune system, lower blood pressure, improved sleep and less stress. So keep the habit of sex with your spouse to keep your relationship strong, and improve your health.

Whichever habits you focus on for your relationship, doing something new is better than not doing anything at all. Keep your relationship a focus in your life, and constantly seek to keep it strong.

Questions & Answers

Identify which habits in your marriage are bad and how can you get rid of them?

_____

_____

_____

_____

_____

Identify which habits in your marriage are healthy ones. Are there ways to make them stronger?

_____

_____

_____

_____

_____

Are there some habits you would like to implement into your marriage to make it stronger?

_____

_____

_____

_____

_____

FAMILY HABITS

There is a saying; you can pick your friends but not your family. Picture this scenario: you're at the park, a child runs into you while you are tying your shoe knocking you backwards on your bottom. The mother is apologetic and the kid is terrified because it was an accident and they don't know how you will react.

Most people will shrug it off; say it's nothing and not a big deal. Picture the same scenario now, but it was your kid who knocked you back. Or your sibling, spouse, parent. You're not as nice, you snap at them, and they feel really bad even though it was clearly an accident. Maybe it's just me, but I know this relates to me, or some kind of scenario like this would.

Most people treat their own family worse than they do strangers. Common courtesy is extended to strangers (which is a GOOD habit) but not to our family which is a bad habit. Most people take family for granted. This is a bad habit and its one of the worst ones when it comes to your family.

If we are to have direction and purpose in our life, we need to have excellent habits that help and serve not only ourselves, but the people around us. Does this mean that we do not have a single bad habit? Of course not, there will always be some bad habits that come into play in our lives. Having good habits is not about having no bad habits, just having more really good ones!

Our habits, whether we realize it or not, are shaping and directing our lives. The bad habits keep us down in the muck and the grim of life, they serve us as a constant reminder that we suck. They are destructive and useless, but without the bad habits we sometimes have, we would not understand what a good habit really is. So next time you treat your family member worse than you would a stranger, pause and think about what really matters.

Good habits shape our lives, they push us in directions we wish to go and get us to the goals we so desperately want to achieve. The good habits are the ones that should be playing the most dominate role in our lives. Try to keep the balance tipped in the favor of the good, especially when it comes to your family. A good habit would be keeping the at-home atmosphere comfortable for all.

A way you can do this is by savoring moments with your family, playing together, working together (not against each other) and each individual seeking to understand before they are understood. When you create that inviting atmosphere for each family member then it lays the ground work for better habits to be brought into the family life.

Things you can do and implement into habits to bring your family closer are having dinner together, family meetings, and having a general routine of habits for the children to expect. Studies have shown when a family sits down together most nights (or every night if possible) that children do better in school, are less likely to suffer from depression and are less likely to consider suicide. The simple habit of eating a meal as a family together can have such a huge impact on your children's future.

Try and implement that habit if you haven't already. Having a family meeting might sound a little silly, but most families have reported back it makes them feel more connected. They give everyone a chance to be heard and work things out when people are calm, and meetings set a great example for your kids to work out problems maturely.

Lastly, having routine most days helps your children out more than one would think. Kids thrive on routines and structure. It makes them feel safe, helps them know what to expect and when, which means it's a little easier on everyone involved. Your daily routine includes the habits you choose to keep, so make sure they are good ones you want your children to see in you. Hopefully you see the sense in these three ideas of habits to implement in your family life, and can think of other good ones to improve on.

Questions & Answers

Is the atmosphere at home welcoming?

_____
_____
_____
_____
_____

What habit do you wish to work on with your family?

_____
_____
_____
_____
_____

What bad habit do you want to get rid of?

_____
_____
_____
_____
_____

What is your plan of action to get rid of said bad habit, or to change it into a good one?

_____
_____
_____
_____

Is there anything you want to change in your routine to improve family life? Do so ASAP!

_____
_____
_____
_____

AT WORK HABITS

To begin on the pathway of developing the best habits we can have in life we need to identify what it is we are attempting to achieve. Our desired results and outcomes will help shape the habit into a productive force with unlimited power for good. If someone wants a promotion at work as a result, they need to hustle at work.

That means staying late, showing up early, taking on responsibilities and being the "go to" individual in the workplace. Does that mean that they will get the promotion? No, it's not a guarantee, but they are way more likely if they are practicing good habits such as the ones mentioned. The said promotion would go to the employee with good habits hopefully before the employee who takes long lunches and leaves early and shows up late, right?

The worst case scenario for the employee with good habits that is seeking a promotion is that individual gets really good at different areas of work and since they did not get promoted, they find a different job where they value the good habits. The point is good habits always pay off in our life.

Promotions at work, a healthy relationship and other various goals are easily attainable when you put into practice good habits. Do not be discouraged when results are not spilling over after one day. The fact remains that it is not a habit after one day!

Habits take time to develop, that goes for the good and the bad. These habits have the power to shape our reality and the time it takes to build up good habits will pay you off in a tremendous way. Forming a good habit that serves your life in a productive way takes time and patience on your part. It takes only 30 days to develop a healthy happy habit that will last a life time!

The word "time" is a four letter word that we do not like to hear. In a world of instant results, spending "time" and being patient for a result sounds like a painfully dull dagger being inserted into your abdomen. The reward far outweighs the pain associated to waiting and being patient.

Let me give you an example that rocks. There are two men, Tony and Ralph, they are both equally strong and are tasked to individually cut down a massive tree with an axe. Ralph goes up to his tree and starts swinging, he is super determined to cut down the tree today and spends all day and finally gives up late into the night.

He wakes up the next day sore and tired but heads to the tree anyways, he starts swinging and stops after a few swings, he decides he will do it tomorrow, he needs to rest. Ralph sleeps in and never goes back to the tree.

Tony goes up to his tree and is determined he will cut down the tree also but only spends a small amount of time chopping away. Tony walks around the tree and analyzes how much he accomplished that day and feels rewarded.

Tony goes back daily until the tree falls.

When we can take small swings at our goal tree each day and then be proud of the progress, we will have far better chances of making it to success. If we on the other hand try to get a final result in one day, we are going to be sorely disappointed and burnt out before we ever find success.

We need to be proud of the small milestones we hit on a daily basis and not just be focused on the end result. If you spend all the time in the world focusing on the end result, if you reach it, you will be less than satisfied.

Anticipation of the result is far greater than the actual result. Have you ever anticipated a new car? A vacation? Anything and then proceeded to get the result? Chances are you have and chances are it was not as spectacular as you built it up in your mind to be. It is normal occurrence that we all do, but should try to avoid. We need to enjoy the small stepping stones of progress towards our successes. This especially applies to work. You don't wake up one day and run a huge successful business, you have to start at the bottom and work your way up. Along the way if you instill great working habits then it will pay off.

A person having a day of good habits makes no logical sense. Habits take time to form into habits and time to develop. That day of good habits is more like a day of good actions. The best way to understand when something becomes a habit is when the action or task no longer requires you to think about it.

Many writers and entrepreneurs of all kinds have gotten in the habit of awaking at the wee hours of the morning. Do people prefer to wake up at 5am? Or do the real crazy ones who do it, prefer to wake up at 4 o'clock in the morning? Of course they do not, but they know it is the only way they can find the extra time they need to work on their goals and aspirations. Benjamin Franklin asked himself daily when he woke up at 5am, "What good shall I do today?" and before bed every evening at about 10pm, "What good have I done today?" Benjamin formed a habit of analyzing himself and reflecting on what he was going to do and what he did every day. This habit kept him in check for his life.

Daily habits such as Benjamin's are designed to help and serve not only the one who holds the habit, but the world around the individual. Our habits shape the world as we know it and when we instill productive and powerful habits, we see the world shape in a way that is beautiful and that is full of endless possibilities.

In order to be productive, you have to analyze your habits and work tendencies you already have established and ingrained.

Step 1: Organize a list of tendencies

Do not lie on this, just be honest and truthful for real results or it will not work. Here's an example to help you for a self-employed graphic designer.

8am – Start Work by Opening Email
8:30am – 10am – Check Facebook, Check News, Read some articles
10am – 12pm – Start working but have Facebook up on a different page checking in once a while
12pm-1pm – Take a lunch break
1pm-5pm – Check email, work, check Facebook

Step 2: Locate Problematic Areas

Benjamin A. Chapin

In the scenario we listed, it's pretty easy to identify the problems that Mr. Graphic Designer is having. If you were to check Facebook 5 times a day for 10 minutes, that's almost an hour of productivity that is lost. In order to combat the distractions, the best course of action is to not have a window or tab open in your browser for them.

Step 3: Organize the Productive Habits

In order to work smarter, not harder, you have to be able to have a system to how you go about your business in a constructive way. An easy way to do this is designate time periods in the day for specific tasks and areas to focus on.

8am – Check Email
8:30am – 12pm – Work on items that need attention then work on attaining new business
12pm – Check Email
1pm – 4:30pm – Work on items that need attention and then work to retain old business
4:30pm – Check Email
5pm – End of Day

Step 4: Never Stop Thinking

In the scenario above or any job that is a career; you never want to shut the lights out on business. Your mind is an excellent problem solver and thinker, let it think. While you are driving, in moments of quiet, let your mind wander over to problems that need solutions with your work.

When you condition your mind to always be in a state of usefulness, by the time you get going on a task, you already know exactly what you want to accomplish and it will help you work smarter every single time you sit down to work.

Game Plan for Productivity

Step 1: Identify How You Spend Your Time Working

Step 2: Locate the Problems in Your Working Time

Step 3: Organize the Productive Items You Do

Step 4: Continue To Think & Plan Ahead

Questions & Answers

Can you identify the bad habits that you have at work?

_____

_____

_____

_____

_____

How can you break the bad habits that are holding you back?

_____

_____

_____

_____

_____

What good habits do you want to add to your work day?

_____

_____

_____

_____

_____

Can you adjust your thinking on any bad habits to help you realize they are actually productive?

_____

_____

_____

_____

_____

SUMMARY OF SECTION 2

When you work on yourself first, you can offer the best of you to the people around you. Your spouse will notice the more confident loving person you've become, and value what you bring to the relationship with the habits you use to bond closer with one another. Paying attention and showing your love in daily actions (habits) will go a long way to the happiness of your relationship.

Your children and family will thrive when you work on building your family up by having dinner together, having family meetings once a week, and having a general routine of habits for the children to expect.

Lastly, your working environment will see how productive you've become and reward you, either with raises or promotions. Great work does not go unrecognized for long. Working on your relationships and productiveness in them is another piece closer to a life full of happiness from having the right kind of habits.

SECTION 3: FINANCIAL HABITS

"The power of your habit is the obsession of your mind" – Benjamin Chapin

In order to get habits into full gear you need to obsess over them in the beginning. The reality of habits is the fact it takes a while to develop them. Thirty days is how long it usually takes to turn that action into a habit. If you have a targeted "good habit" and you do it once or twice, is it a habit? The answer is simply no.

Obsession has a rather negative persona when it comes up in conversations. The word is usually used describe someone that has a problem.

"Sally was obsessed with that boy and that's why it didn't end up working out"

"John is obsessed with his job; he works long hours and is neglecting his family"

"Susan was obsessed with that television show"

"I swear she is obsessive compulsive"

All the above quotes are common use with the word obsess. One of the definitions of "obsessive" is "all-consuming" or "fanatic". When thinking on terms of good habits, do you think changing your life dramatically and breaking down bad habits to make them good requires the one making the change to be a little fanatic or all consumed?

The answer is all consumed. You need to be in it for the long haul, and really want the change. You have to want the results more then you want the temporary pleasure of the bad habit. Sometimes this involves pointing out how damaging or stressful the bad habit is.

One of the biggest stresses in life is financial stress. But if you take a step back, reflect over your spending habits, saving habits, and then work on some budgeting habits you will be more stress-free than you ever realized you could be. If you start off and let your budget consume you while grasping what living in your means is, then you will have a clearer idea on what you can spend and what you need to save.

Questions & Answers

Do you feel like you live within your means?

_____
_____
_____
_____
_____

Do you over spend?

_____
_____
_____
_____
_____

Do you under save?

_____
_____
_____
_____
_____

Do you think you have enough in savings?

_____
_____
_____
_____
_____

SPENDING HABITS

"An over-indulgence of anything, even something as pure as water, can intoxicate." ~ Criss Jami

Bad habits hold people back from accomplishing a myriad of goals, desires and dreams. The bad habit is toxic and should be eliminated or at least adjusted to be a more productive useful habit. The great news about them is the fact they can be easily identified in our lives and can be broken.

The bad habit takes what you want in life and keeps you finger lengths away from them. In order to eliminate these habits, we need to analyze them at a close range. Let's use the common bad habit that some people have that is toxic, the dreaded bad spending habit.

The bad spending habit plays a critical role in the downfall of many people's finances. In order to adjust the habit, we have to drill down to the core of the issue. The issue is not that they are spending money on un-needed stuff, but they are acting impulsively and are seeking instant gratification of some sort.

Why does this person need to spend? What is driving them to this habit? Where did it start out and was there an issue that triggered this habit to take form. The core issue could already be resolved, but the person is still stuck in the habit.

Oftentimes, there is a void that a person is trying to fill when they spend irresponsibly, other times they are just immature and did not know any better. Regardless of why it began, the change can only be made when the individual with the bad habit can acknowledge the toxicity that is associated with the bad habit.

Trying to change someone else and their habits will never work. If you were thinking down that direction, stop, I've been there and it is not a productive road. In fact, that itself is a bad habit. You cannot change people or their habits.

In order to overcome the bad habit and make an adjustment, you have to find the gold nugget that is inside every habit, good or bad. In the example of the bad spending habit, the individual that is spending can adjust the bad habit for good. This transformation will require a lot of strength depending on how far the habit trails back to its origination.

We will speculate on the bad spending habit individual that they are buying clothing at "rock bottom" prices and very obsessed with bargains and deals. Instead of focusing on clothing and shopping on un-needed stuff, they can harness that power and direct it towards their grocery needs. Everybody needs groceries and if they can direct that focus and determination into their grocery spending, they can satisfy that need to spend but in a productive way.

As mentioned previously, this requires people to shed

away the "absolute truths" that are ever present. Individuals who have the bad habit of spending need to shed away the fact that they love to shop for clothes and that is just part of who they are. When we can break our bond to the bad habits we have, we can make the needed adjustments for some good habits like shopping for food instead of clothes (unless clothes are actually needed in the case of old clothes worn out or grown out of).

Living within Your Means is something many people need to get a handle on. If you can't afford groceries at the end of a paycheck, you certainly don't need to be eating out right when you get paid. If you cannot afford your electric bill, you don't need cable. If you can't afford a high car payment, do not trade in your old paid off car and get a new one! No one is impressed when you can't pay your bills, no matter how cool you think you look. If you live humble and in your means you will save money and have less stress financially. Your relationships will have huge improvements when finances are not an issue. All around it is a huge benefit to be wise about your money.

Habits to implement in your spending life:
1.   Making a monthly budget. Write down bills first, then essential extras. Make sure to add a little into savings each check.
2.   Make a weekly meal plan (work your way up to a monthly meal plan and buy in bulk to save money). Having meals planned ahead decreases the chance you will eat out spontaneously and waste money.
3.   Grocery shop with a list and stick to it, only take enough money for your list.
4.   Clip coupons, and price match. If you don't have time to price match, Wal-Mart has an application for phones where you can scan your receipt and it price matches for you. If they find a lower advertised price they will give you the money back! So simple and easy to save.

There are many phone applications out there where all you have to do is scan your receipt and it will give you money back. Some are called Checkout51, Snap, and Target has an application called Cartwheel where you scan your barcode while checking out and it takes off the coupons you have added to it. Most grocery stores have websites you can add coupons to your store card. So be sure to check out those options to save extra money.

5.   If you are going shopping for clothes or gifts, take cash out of your bank or ATM for what you have budgeted, and leave credit/debit cards AT HOME. There are too many appealing items out there, last minute buys that we really don't need and later will regret.

6.   Pack your lunch instead of eating out every day. Instead of spending that $10 a day on a sandwich, chips and a drink make it at home and bring it instead. Spend maybe $4 packing your lunch and save $6 a day. That adds up pretty quick at $30 a week, $120 a month, and up to $1,500 a year!

7.   Save before you spend. We will talk about building your savings up first before making big purchases and splurging in the next chapter.

Here is a sample budget to help you write out your own:

(This person brings home $2,127 a month or about $531 a week)

Monthly Bills:
Vehicle payment $130
Vehicle insurance $122
Rent/Morgage $800
Renters Insurance $10
Electric $112
Water/Gas $103
Cell Phone $50

Grocery money $400 ($100 a week)
Vehicle Gas Money $200 ($50 a week)
Savings $100
Extra $100

If you live within what you have budgeted, then you won't have the stress of late payments or bill collectors. You will be able to have a holiday without taking out a loan or borrowing money. I once heard a woman tell me she only gets her kids four things for Christmas.

1. Something to wear
2. Something to read
3. Something they want
4. Something they need

Instead of buying tons of toys and clothes that they don't always need, I urge people to think about cutting back. We want our children to be happy, but we also want them to grow up appreciating life and being thankful for what they do get, not mad because they didn't get the latest gadget from the store.

Questions & Answers

What is your weakness when it comes to spending?

_____

_____

_____

_____

_____

What spending can you cut back on?

_____

_____

_____

_____

_____

Write out a budget for this month.

_____

_____

_____

_____

_____

Get a monthly budget guide FREE when you request your gift. (see resource section)

SAVING HABITS

Most people do not have enough money saved. They live paycheck to paycheck, and this is a bad habit. Here are some ideas to start your savings account even if you are living paycheck to paycheck.

Step 1: You have to know your expenses.

Take your budget you wrote out in the last chapter and see where you can squeeze out $5 to put into your savings account. Do that the first month. For the second month put $20 into savings. An idea to earn that money is to take a survey online and then put the money into savings. For the next month, put $50 away; sell some old items lying around the house if you can't squeeze it out of your budget. Next month put $100, doing the various extra activities to earn your savings. By doing a little extra each month with surveys, selling unused items, you can keep your regular paycheck for bills in your budget. If you continue to save you will feel so much better having that extra in the bank!

Step 2: Save at least a year's expenses.

Most recessions last under 12 months, so if you have saved enough to cover all your expenses for a year, then you can feel better about splurging on items you have earned after all your hard work. Or taking that vacation you always wanted.

Step 3: Resist upgrades!

Most do not have a years' worth of expenses saved, most are lucky if they have a month! So to resist spending on things you don't need and upgrades on things you already have here are some questions to ask yourself.

1. Do you NEED it to survive?
2. You have gone this far without it so why is it so important?
3. Can you wait? Most items are way over priced when they first come out. Wait a couple months or even a year and then you can get that item you HAD to have at a discount! Or you will find that item wasn't as important as you thought it was.

When we identify the bad habits, we can break them by rewiring our brains. The problematic spender will need to break the bad habit by wiring a new habit. The old habit will still have connections wired up in the brain, but it will no longer be used after the new habit is in place.

Habits are similar to a freeway; there are multiple freeways to get you where you want to go. In order to take the right freeway, we have to understand the direction and destination we are attempting to get to. If we do not like the freeway, we build a new one.

Instead of getting a crew and laying new roads down, you are getting a new habit (freeway) and you just keep taking that route to your destination. It's all in the mind and it is all about the connections we make in our mind. Use your mind to do away with the bad habits of overspending and under saving, and develop these new habits to make life easier and stress free financially.

Questions & Answers

What areas can you save on in your budget?

_____

_____

_____

_____

_____

What are some things you can do to earn extra money this month?

_____

_____

_____

_____

_____

Write out a plan for putting money into savings each month.

_____

_____

_____

_____

_____

Take your plan and put it to action. Watch those numbers add up!

SUMMARY OF SECTION 3

Living within your means makes it so you are stress free finically for daily living. Having a savings account that you regularly put money into gives you security for the twists life throws at everyone. Writing out a monthly budget makes a huge difference in how successful these new habits will be, so be sure to write it out how you can understand it.

Changing your spending and saving habits into good ones while following a budget is something you need to start TODAY, and it's a good idea to bring it up at that weekly family meeting habit that we talked about starting in section 2. Good luck, I know you can do it.

SECTION 4: LIFE TRANSFORMED

Life is truly changed when you transform your old bad habits into new healthier ones. When you eat better and work out, you feel improved and interact with everyone around you better. They will appreciate the happy, healthy you instead of the grumpy, tired, old you.

When you don't over spend, but save money instead your financial stress is gone. By not having financial stress you will even FEEL healthier. Studies show finical stress doesn't just affect your wallet but it affects your health, so two HUGE motivations to keep up with the good habits we've hopefully started to implement from reading this book!

Living within your means now creates benefits throughout your entire life. Choose lasting happiness from good habits over temporary happiness of bad ones. Your good habits will build you and your loved ones a good life. Keep your eyes on the prize and I know you can stay determined and in it for the long haul!

Now you know the areas of your life that habits can

make positive or negative impact, now follow me as I give you some additional information into how to make those habits easier to attain and additional habits of successful people that can change your life.

BATCH AND AUTOMATION

"A nail is driven out by another nail; habit is overcome by habit." ~
Desiderius Erasmus

Time management is something everyone can work on
a little. Finding time to add these new habits to life is a
concern that we don't take lightly, so if you batched some
parts of your life it will make it easier on you. An example
of baking cookies can illustrate what I am talking about.
How interesting would it be if someone cooked a single
chocolate chip cookie at a time? Just one normal sized
cookie dropped onto the cookie sheet and baked for the 8-
12 minutes. Let us take it a step further and say they need
to make 4 dozen cookies.

If each cookie takes 10 minutes to bake, the process of
4 dozen cookies will take about 8 hours. We do not bake
cookies individually though, we like to bake them a dozen
at a time. So instead of 8 hours, we get them done in 40
minutes. The time saved between the two is tremendous.

Just as we batch our favorite cookies, we can also batch
particular aspects of our lives. View certain blocks of time
as the cookie sheet and the tasks as the cookie dough. The

tasks we have slated to do daily can all be done in one block of time for maximum efficiency.

Instead of debating if I should shower before I make coffee or if I should do this before that in the morning, I tossed everything into a batch habit and now it works like clockwork. I do not need to adjust or change anything unless I am out of town or if I move. The rest of the time it's the exact same every single day.

Batching the mundane and repetitive tasks helps free the mind to think and clearly setup what it needs to focus on for the day. No longer are the moments of "should I take a shower now or wait until I drink this cup of coffee", these little moments take the focus of the mind and reduces productivity with other more pressing matters that are at hand.

The more pressing matters at hand are the items that you cannot batch and put on your cookie sheet. They are the new problems you need to solve for the day, they are what you are going to do today to make the day useful. A nice relaxing day of doing nothing can sound delightful, but they leave you with a sense of uselessness.

Who wants to be useless? Of course, we all need a break from the lives we live and those breaks are useful and refreshing for our minds and are essential for our lives. However, a useless day that is spoken of is a day in which serves no purpose. The kind of day where at the end of it, you think to yourself that day was a waste.

Batching frees the mind to be more productive and useful, no longer having the focus re-directed to meaningless mundane tasks, the mind will be able to clearly steer your life where you want to go. The mind is the most precious tool we will ever own and is essentially in setting up batching in a successful manner.

Morning rituals are not the only area of life that can be batched. Healthy working habits can be batched into blocks of time also. If you need to accomplish A, B and C at work you have a variety of choices outside of a batching.

You might spend the morning doing A and then do some C and then back to A then over to B. Trying to juggle it all together randomly depending on how time permits. Instead of doing this, develop a batched system of habits that prove more productive.

Work on "A" until it is finished, then work on "B" and when that is done work on "C". The concept is easy, but can be difficult to adapt in real world scenarios. Let us do a real world scenario for these letters and develop the concept with a little more depth.

You arrive in the office at 9:00 am; "A" will represent the urgent pressing matters from the previous day. You will work on them, ignoring new issues that might arise "B", once you finish up the pressing matters "A"; you begin to work on "B" if applicable and then "C" which is email. Of course, if some critical "need it done yesterday" comes into the mix, you will need to focus on that, but then you can immediately return to the task at hand.

The goal here with the habit of batching is to keep everything organized within the time you have at work. The batched task management system you develop will save yourself a lot of pain and headaches. Often in work places you see people become overwhelmed because they do not know where to start with what they need to do.

The people who feel overwhelmed with work have two possible scenarios. The first being thinking they are being overworked and over extended, in this case they will burn out and are likely to quit. The second scenario is an individual with a habit of batching. If they develop a systematic batching habit, they will relieve the stress ball they feel inside.

The problem is oftentimes people will check their email "C" and even "D" which was not even on the list, such as Facebook, News Websites and so on. Then, the work starts to pick up and they have a variety of different options to start with. They already are feeling unproductive sitting on Facebook, so they end up not doing much of anything and waste an afternoon at work.

The distractions we have keep our priorities out of whack and exhaust our mental strength. When we can develop a good healthy habit of batching coupled with other good habits, we can be more productive in all the work we do.

Tim Ferris in the "Four Hour Work Week" mentions batching your email. He says to check email at specific set times in the day. The goal by doing this is to increase efficiency and not be reading emails randomly all through the day.

While I agree with Tim's philosophy on email, I do believe the concept cannot be adapted at all times. Oftentimes there are people in job roles that cannot be away from email for a moment, it's literally part of their job to be able to respond quickly. So it does not work for everyone.

There are areas of life that should never be batched for relieving the mind of thinking. Batching family activities and conversations with loved ones should not be approached in the same manner. Batching is to make the repetitive un-important tasks more systematic, it is not designed to put your relationships on autopilot. Habits can be created and formed for relationships, but not batching habits.

The purpose of batching is to free your mind of clutter and ridiculous decision making that does not need the input of your mind. When you master batching and adapt it to your way of life, the power of you gain is unsurpassable. The mind is cleaned of un-needed thinking and is more apt to think on things that have substance and meaning.

In order to set up your good habits to run automatically there is a bit of leg work required until they are established. Good habits do not develop overnight; they also do not take form by doing them every once in a while.

It all begins within the mind. The mind is the powerhouse that is running and directing your life. It makes all the decisions and choices and many of them in the matter of mere seconds. To setup the new habits to automatically run, you'll need to tap into those split second decisions your mind makes.

To do this, it will require you to force upon your mind that these new habits are part of who you are now. Doing so will require yourself to force your focus onto that new habit and show it being performed. The reason why it takes a month to form a habit is because the mind has to write new wiring in the brain.

If you have a desire to not spend money on clothing, your mind will need to re-write the part of your brain that automatically gravitates towards purchasing clothing you find appealing. Identify the automatic tendencies you already have and adjust them to your new habits if applicable. For example, if you are turning that clothing shopping habit into grocery shopping bargains, let the piece of clothing you see trigger that new grocery habit.

You might have the thought "That's a nice shirt, I wonder how much it is..." use that thought to trigger "I wonder what discounts they have in their weekly ad for meats." How can you make this change? This change can be accomplished by being made aware like you are being made aware right now.

In order to make a shift, you have to know what you are shifting and where to look for it at. The fact you are reading this is right now means that your mind is processing new information to make you more aware of these automatic habits and it will help you remember to make the changes. You still have to push yourself and your mind to actively perform the habits daily.

What our mind does not do is simply give up on automatic reactions and triggers without being pressed upon what to do instead. The wiring in the mind for the old bad habits do not dissolve, they are ever present, so we need to make sure the new wiring is used instead.

Questions & Answers

What areas do you already have "batching" in place for?

_____
_____
_____
_____
_____

Are there areas of your life you can reduce or eliminate the need to think (batch more)?

_____
_____
_____
_____
_____

Could you institute a routine of batching in a new area of your life in order to take the load off of your mind?

_____
_____
_____
_____
_____

What do you think of automation and the ease it provides for your life?

_____
_____
_____
_____
_____

THE SUCCESS CONNECTION

"Just do it! First you make your habits, then your habits make you!" ~
Lucas Remmerswaal

Finding success with every part of your life should be a goal that everybody has. How wonderful would it be if you had the best health, the best marriage, the best job and every single person you knew respected you and loved you? That's insane to think that could all fit into reality, but it is not insane one bit.

If you condition your mind to believe you are successful and get into the habit of "patting yourself on the back" you will find success. You have to know and realize you are already successful and also still achieve more success. They call it being content but always striving for more.

Vince Lombardi put it this way, "Strive for perfection, settle for excellence." How poetic and true when it comes to good habits and finding success. Your habits run your life, if you have habits revolved around watching television, playing video games and working the bare minimum at work; you will not advance in life.

Successful people have successful habits that keep them ahead of the game and excelling more. The more success they find, the more fuel they have to keep rising to the top. The first step is always the most difficult, but once you start it's hard for you to stop.

Finding success in all we do is only difficult when we are starting out. If you set out to make a goal and come up short, count your winnings and see where you can adjust to get a better result next time. Having the habit of never admitting defeat but continuously striving will keep the fuel in your belly lit and your passion on fire towards your goals and overall results you are attempting to hit.

Let us go over the habits that some of the most successful people have and that have been steering them to successful lives for many years.

Habit 1: Be Proactive

We have to get into a state and habit of actively taking care of business and concerns. Instead of running around putting fires out, we should already have the grass wet and avoid the fires. Actively seeking problematic issues and tackling them before they get a chance to get up and fight you is the basic goal here.

This requires us to have the ability to tackle things that need to be done before they turn into headaches and problems. If that means cutting down the excess and focusing more on a particular area, you need to make that shift.

Oftentimes our lives get over-consumed and we are stretched fifty different directions that all we can actively do is run from one issue to the next. There is no time to be proactive in that environment and we have to fix the problem or get ourselves out of it.

Once we resolve the issues and trim off the fat that does not allow us to focus in on our area of responsibility, we are able to be proactively seeking, resolving everything within the given area and thus nurturing the habit of being proactive.

Habit 2: Begin with the End in Mind

Basic goal setting on everything we are doing is going to accomplish this habit. I personally like to set goals continuously and daily, I need to accomplish A, B, C today and D, E & F a little bit later. Having the end in your mind's eye will help steer the boat in that direction.

If you have a ship in the harbor and just loose it from the port, it'll float around and bump into other stuff on its way out, and without any instructions or guidance, the boat will float around randomly until it hits some piece of land. That's no way to direct a boat and we shouldn't approach our daily lives and tasks that way either.

It's going to benefit us greatly if we can just simply know where we are going and what we are trying to accomplish with what we are doing in the moment. If I'm baking a pie, I want to eat it. It's simple, but it works and has been done by successful people for a long time.

Habit 3: Put First Things First

Having a sense of order about your habits and your life is essential. If you realize you are spending time on something that is unproductive, stop doing it. Staying focused on your priorities is a key component in success. Keeping a sense of order is a habit that provides value on a daily basis throughout life.

Habit 4: Think Win/Win

Always keeping in mind others and yourself for every deal you strike is a habit of gold. You cannot find success on a continuous basis if you are only taking and you cannot find it if you are only giving. A healthy habit of Give and Take in everything you do is going to benefit your life in a variety of ways and should always be practiced.

Habit 5: Seek First to Understand, Then to be Understood

Nothing kills a moment quicker than someone running their mouth about something they have no clue about. Getting into the habit of understanding before you start on the path is the key to being able to not only execute but have people understand what you are doing.

If you speak without understanding first, you come across as ignorant and have no clue to what you are doing. You will find yourself hard pressed to have people join your vision if you are constantly talking about stuff you have no clue about.

Maintaining a habit of understanding before you seek to be understood is an ace in your hand every time.

Habit 6: Synergize

You being an army of one will not be the way to succeed in life. You have to find other people that help push you towards your goals. Synergizing and playing on strengths of those around you and the contacts you acquire along the way are going to take you way farther than anything you do on your own.

The strength of many will always out-weigh the strength of one. It is okay to connect with other people and use them. They will use you also. The habit of strengthening others and using their strengths will take you far in your path to success.

Habit 7: Sharpen the Saw

In order to keep production levels high and the quality of what is being produced, you have to find a balance between that which is productive and that which is beneficial to your life. That means developing a balance of your productive life and the other areas that interest you. You have to have time for physical, mental, social, emotional and spiritual and taking a break from the production is needed.

Getting in the habit of balancing between your personal life and your productive life is difficult at first, you might be super obsessed with your goals and plans on production, but neglecting the other side will cause ramifications to the other. The habit of balancing will sharpen your production to new heights.

These habits are success habits that can morph and direct your life in the direction you want to go. They can also be played off in order to create different habits in your own life. Whatever it is you desire, you can achieve by instituting these habits.

Practicing the success habits will take some time. Each habit you want to create can take around thirty days or so to develop. Be patient and strong in building your good habits and breaking the bad and you will get there.

Once the habits are formed, they will take on their own

lives and show you how to direct your life. Instead of forcing yourself into adapting the habits to situations, you will just act without thought. Eventually you will no longer need to think your mind will just direct you with the new habits because they have become a part of who you are.

Questions & Answers

Do you believe you can find success in all areas of life with good habits?

_____

_____

_____

_____

_____

Do you already or do you plan to have a mindset of "Strive for perfection, Settle for excellence" when it comes to your habits? Why or why not?

_____

_____

_____

_____

_____

Which of the seven habits of successful people stood out to you? Why or why not?

_____

_____

_____

_____

_____

Do you understand how powerful habits are and how they direct your life now?

_____

_____

_____

_____

_____

SUMMARY OF SECTION 4

When you batch the mundane tasks you have in your everyday life, you will see improvements across the board. Your mind is arguably one of the fundamental building blocks of building good habits and without it; you would be in the dark. Easing the burden on your mind allows you to easily achieve your goals and aspirations you have in your life. Adapting and changing the behaviors of your routines is going to excel that to the next level.

Cultivating habits for success is going to get your life moving in the right direction and put you on the fast track for success. Following through on your new habits and modifying your older ones is going to give you the edge you need to get everything moving forward.

CONCLUSION

Our habits in life shape our reality and reflect our mental health on a daily basis. It is only when we are able to identify, adjust, and change our habits that we can release the true power that is within each habit. This power, once realized, will help you make the changes to your habits and you will lead a healthier life. Healthier living like eating right and exercising regularly provides outstanding benefits that make it worth it to change and become the best version of you possible.

When you work on yourself first, you can offer the best of you to the people around you. Your relationship with your spouse will improve on just the extra attention you are dedicating to improving it. They notice the little things! Your children and family with thrive with the different habits we've talked about to build the bonds of family up and each other. Family is so important. Last of all, your working environment will see how productive you've become and reward you, either with raises or promotions. Great work does not go unrecognized for long.

Living a life free of stress is rare, but if you know how much you make and how much you need to save before you spend then you will be that much closer to a stress free life. How great would that be? Remember to regularly put money into your savings account to give yourself security for the twists life throws at everyone.

Batching different aspects of our lives makes it easier to find time to implement these great habits, so think about what areas you can batch and start doing it. Remember the story of baking cookies to help visualize batching different things in your day. Never forget when there is a will, there is a way. We are realistic in the knowledge that this all won't happen overnight, but optimistic that you can accomplish the habits we've talked about in this book.

Enjoy how your life has been transformed from breaking away from old bad habits and making way for the best new habits!

BONUS CHAPTER: STEP 1
DISCOVERED THOUGHT LIFE

"The greatest discovery of all time is that a person can change his future by merely changing his attitude." ~ Oprah Winfrey

The act of "thinking" is something that comes so naturally to us that we often do not even think about it. Our thoughts are the single most powerful influence we have on the direction of our life. To make the transformation over to a positive thinking life, we have to understand the dynamics of our thinking first. Did you know that a single thought, a single decision in your life can change the course of your existence?

Years ago while my wife and I were dating long distance (ouch I know!) we fought about issues we had and didn't really have very good conversations. One day, my wife prompted me with a question—well, an ultimatum—which was: I was either to drop the petty topics about ex-boyfriends or she's done. After a quick 5 second moment of thought, I quickly agreed to drop it and the problem was solved.

I decided not to let my thoughts focus there. That 5 second decision of thought rippled through my entire life. I ended up relocating to her state, marrying her, and starting our life together. Understanding the role our thoughts play is crucial to living happy, successful, and enjoyable lives.

Humans share many of the same desires. We desire to be important, wealthy, happy, and stress-free in our daily life. The key to making this a reality has nothing to do with money, nothing to do with the amount of friends or status at the country club; it has to do with what we think about and dwell on.

The results we see in our life are in direct correlation with the thoughts we process. What we dwell on, what we focus on, what we pursue all comes into existence before our eyes. When you spend your time focused on the good in life and what brings you peace, happiness, and joy, you will output what you take into your mind.

The bible mentions it a few times, "a man reaps what he sows." What you plant into your mind you will end up reaping from it, whether it's good or bad. Newton's Third Law states "For every action, there is an equal and opposite reaction."

An example of Newton's law is when we direct our mind to push forward into positive thinking, we will move forward. People have influences and direction coming into their mind through the media, books, magazines, friends, family, and co-workers. Even strangers we are passing by in the supermarket or on the sidewalk can be an influence that enters the mind.

What we spend our time day dreaming about and focused

on is an indicator of the direction in which we are going. If we think about nothing, we will become nothing. Recognizing the negative influences in our thinking life is a good step towards changing our thinking, but it's only the beginning of the journey.

Gaining control over your thoughts is not as easy as it sounds, there isn't an app for that, but the good news is it also isn't too difficult once you gain experience and practice in doing it. Practice makes perfect, even when it comes to our thoughts. Not only that, you'll actually start enjoying the process when you see your positive thoughts effortlessly manifesting themselves into your reality on a daily basis.

Gaining control over your thoughts means gaining control over your life. With everything that happens to you being a product of your thoughts and beliefs, thoughts are simply a preview of what's up next in your life. Think of it as a movie trailer; you don't know what the movie is exactly like, but you have a pretty good idea of what it will be about.

It's the same with thoughts. Your thinking life determines your reality. If you have negative thoughts, fears, paranoia, etc. all of them lead to negative results, which end up being your reality.

Are you beginning to see how your thoughts are powerful? The fact is, the power you have to control your life is unsurpassable. Amplify this power by gaining control over your thoughts and you will start controlling and creating your reality as you see fit.

You have the power to change the course of your life and choose your path. Do not fall victim to the world of social conditioning. Don't succumb to the pressure to be "normal," which is a facade. Who determines what normal is?

Social conditioning is the old school mindset of "fit in or die." When dinosaurs roamed the earth, we had to stick together in groups or we would surely die. Somehow, that train of thought has made it to the modern day and people love to blend in with the crowd.

The problem with blending in is that most people don't have control over their thoughts and more importantly, their life. Chances are you've already blended, but that's okay— you can now see through the curtains of propaganda and mainstream media, and think for yourself. Gain control of your mind, your thoughts, and your behavior.

Having control over your thoughts will enable you to experience true bliss and lasting happiness. You don't have to live your life in a daze going through the motions every day; make life like you've always wanted it to be. It's important to always remember that you have the power to change the course of your life forever by simple thoughts.

Question & Answer

At the end of every chapter there will be some question and answer time, it's just to keep you thinking and keeping some of the topic/challenges fresh in your mind.

How often do you think about the direction your life is going?

How powerful do you see your thoughts to be right now?

Do you see yourself as a positive person?

RESOURCES

Get the free resource as a special thank you for your purchase.

Just visit: http://bit.ly/1A5ttev

OTHER BOOKS

Chronicles Of Kilix (Free Book)

Directional Thinking

Thinking By Design

The Power Of Now

Failing Upwards

Find More Books by Benjamin online

and

Subscribe to the Newsletter

www.benjaminchapin.com

ABOUT THE AUTHOR

BENJAMIN ALLEN CHAPIN is a newer author. Benjamin has in-depth knowledge, experience and expertise in problem solving and thinking clearly. Through years of research and personal experience Benjamin has a message to share with the world. Benjamin lives in Idaho Falls, Idaho with his wife and step daughter. He is a born again Christian who seeks to bring positive light in a sometimes dismal world.

Printed in Great Britain
by Amazon